The Difficult Farm

The Difficult Farm
by Heather Christle

Octopus Books
Denver, Colorado/Portland, Oregon

OCTOPUS
BOOKS

The Difficult Farm
© 2009 Heather Christle

Second edition, 2010
ISBN: 978-0-9801938-4-8
Printed & bound in the USA

Cover design by Denny Schmickle
www.dennyschmickle.com

Octopus Books
Denver, Colorado & Portland, Oregon
www.octopusbooks.net

for my sister

CONTENTS

1

IT'S NOT A GOOD SHORTCUT
IF EVERYONE DIES

Yesterday, looking at a cinderblock's
reflection—lightest grey on golden floor—
I finally understood painting. I was irate!
I took a sledgehammer to the cinderblock,
but as it was supporting the terrarium,
I smashed that as well, and the floor was badly
damaged and the walls weakened, and running
outside to see my house collapse, I finally
understood architecture. I was irate! I went
door to door, to my neighbors, trying to explain
the system we actually inhabit, and they became
absorbed, so we all flapped our arms together
and though we did not fly away I finally
understood how geese make decisions. I was
crushed. I wandered the earth for eighteen years,
honking at anyone who'd listen and there were
a few who even fell in love with me, but because
they did not understand I was under a powerful
spell they could not help me, so I walked sadly
north, migrating so slowly I never reached
anywhere, and in my deceleration I finally
understood infinity's paradox and I myself began
to shrink until my head was too small to contain
much of anything—I'm down to quarks, an idea
so tiny it's sometimes not even there and it suits
me—I appear, the thought appears: quark.

WHAT IS THE CROUP

Monday evening I took out
the garbage. Nobody

saw me, but I looked beautiful.
The last time somebody saw me

I said hello. We were standing up.
I had finished all my chores or

there were one or two left. Darning,
needlepoint, darning. You could

compare my hand to a bobbin
or else another thing. Like you

I live in the area. I live
on the second floor. Even

though our altitudes mismatch
I hope you will think of me.

A good time to think of me
is now. You could say that

is controlling in the English
language. People say things

all the time. Listen in, they
are rotating purses. You can

hear the silk trading hands.
In my brain I use the town hall

as a landmark and then I make
my way. In my way I am

keeping an order. I killed
the insect after I was born.

VARIATIONS ON AN ANIMAL KINGDOM

People love to come up to me and say
Hello, you enormous, vibrating bird,
but they are just confusing me
with my invention, an invention
I regret. Yesterday a whole tree
emptied itself at once and my garden
was large, sad and full of evidence.
You can do so many bad things
and it is so easy. It takes only
a little research and 90% perspiration.
It takes funding and love for the thrush.
People like to say that when I issue
apologies like this it only teaches
others how to modify birds
to their liking. I say very little
for the most part because I am
shaking and very hungry all the time.
It's like there is an actual alarm clock
in my ribcage. It's like an angry harp.
I drive, I use turn signals, and I am always
going off and the birds are always
going off and name for me one town
that isn't trembling. How can I help
but love the whole stupid planet?
In which I make mistakes.
In which growing occurs almost daily,

for those who don't expire. For you
I would make an entirely new animal,
perhaps a larger, more polite bee.
It is very clear to me that I will never
learn my lesson. And that when I am
the one who expires it will help science
begin to mend its injured wings.
I am trying so hard to retire.
I am trying not to steer the wheel
toward the most attractive siderail
I have seen so far today. Sidereal's
a term one has to use and I can
understand that. But this is not
a distance. This is a televised
attempt to bring myself to justice.
A way of reaching up to touch again
the harmless, feral sky. I won't stoop
to demonstrate the birds' small and frantic
black eyes, but you can probably
imagine and then probably stop.

THE CABINET'S ADVICE

It seems sad, and maybe wrong, that there should be this
    many animals,
but not much can be done—it would be too embarrassing
    to get caught

mid-extermination, so effortful, because they are
    everywhere, like the news,
and often as disheartening. This is what it's like to suddenly
    realize that

everyone has a sister, that her hair is going white and curly
    and like so many
of the zoo's exhibits it is very pretty, but inconvenient and
    disruptive

to the original schedule. We should at least try to calm
    down. I once knew
a man who never cleaned his ears, and as a result they
    were just draped

in flowers—hollyhocks, rhododendrons, whatever you'd
    care to imagine.
His hearing wasn't precisely impaired, but rather "over
    there," as if the bells

to which he harkened ran parallel to one's own, so he was
    never lonely, just happy
at a remove. Perhaps, like me, you prefer blueprints to
    architects, a thudding

toe shoe to the glancing ankle it torments. The important
   thing's to demonstrate
that you do, as a human, have adequate desires, but to
   smudge it all enough

to indicate only the general area and not the over-
   cathected dot. People
are inviting you into their living room for the next four
   hours, and so

you have to make them trust you, by the strategic opening
   of humble and personal
vents. Keep in mind the thought that's already been
   nesting there and paying off

the mortgage—a little mistake can lend a sweetness to
   the monument's
unveiling, give poignant entry to the story as you'd rather
   have it told.

9

THEMSELVES PERFORMING
SMALL BRAVE ACTS

I will not renounce anything
for more than eighteen minutes.
I don't want to; I want
to get changed in my bedroom
behind a Japanese screen.
I will not renounce the decorative.
So many lamps have made
me visible to strangers
and where are they now?
The strangers.
I miss them on the side.
There are a million places
I would like to insert my head.
I easily embarrass.
I fear the discovery of our wrongs.
Things melt, then we mop them
and need not make admissions.
I won't renounce the planet
over which a family's scattered. *disconnection*
Relatives are small green dots.
Like other things they are glowing.
Sometimes they move around.
I will sit in a furniture showroom
and watch a hollow phone.
I will sit there and watch it forever.
I will not renounce the sea.

NOT MY NATIVE TONGUE

I would love to undress you.
I suspect underneath
the zipper you are
no less than gold,
that you emit a fat
bold light. That in sleep
you curl up completely,
a red plastic fish.
Look at you flickering.
And it means you are stubborn.
It means you are constant.
It means your little dance.
If I spoke Russian, dearest,
I would say to you
From whom did you receive a letter?
Who was wearing a pretty dress?
What's new? What does this word mean?
What are you writing?
What happened?
Nothing to live on.
I feel like sleeping.
You feel like sleeping.
We feel like going to the movies.

INDIVIDUAL PORTIONS

Just as suddenly it was over and I felt
like an old sheet someone had dropped
into the river, and which had not yet sunk,
but drifted with blue shadows in the largest
of its creases. The river itself resembled
the wooden roads they did not discover
until someone remembered to look down
from orbiting space, and then modern-day
England had to start thinking hard
about the wide-ranging work of the Druids.
Nobody knows what the Druids were like.
When you peel the silk off an ear of corn
you look as though you are sabotaging
a maypole, but also contemplative,
like a stone that's reached old age in a field
of modified poppies. The birthday cake
you did not prepare for me bore a likeness
to the infamous Sarah Morgan, who moved
to town one summer, but never arrived
at school, despite the exquisite sharpness
of the pencils we had readied in hopes
of dazzling our unfamiliar friend. This was
a mystery, much like the night I spent
wallpapering the parlor without you.
Now fourteen feet underwater, I am
still replete with questions: Whose parlor
was it? And why did I work alone?

WHAT AN UNDERTAKER DOES
TO HIS FAMILY AT NIGHT

What an undertaker does to his family at night
cannot be spoken of in man's paraphasic tongue.
For that we need actual metal. Steel signs
arranged by giants. We expect them any minute.
We can hear them sighing and soiling
themselves behind the great mountain.
Compared to the undertaker they lack a career.
Most of the world gets embroidered in the end.
We know that. It's a fact we carry around
like a small sack of seeds with a hole.
Most of our lives get forgotten. It's an assignment,
a motherhood that can't be avoided. I'm not Catholic.
Episcopalian poets control the future from 1953.
Which is the reason for houses. When I'm born
the whole world's born with me. And time
contained in a button. My first trip to the moon,
then my last. I almost stayed there, but then
I remembered Earth's need for new rocks.
I tugged the string and came sputtering back into air.
I have never attended a baseball game, but I understand
it is the only place on this continent where I could
finally stop lying and sleep. I apologize to anyone.
Darling offspring, terrible in Butte, I don't believe in you.
If you're under a sheet, you're a ghost. If you're under
my feet, you're a plant in a poem by an Episcopalian poet.
During the first wireless era, department stores moved
information from one area to another in canisters

shot through pneumatic tubes. That is how I travel.
There are times I'd like to be perfect, i.e. digital.
Other times my knees and elbows are brass and
Catholic poets from 1910 are polishing me. Years ago
at parties we tried to touch people for as long as we could.
Strangers. Once we stood on their couch to sing
the national anthem. My favorite kind of singing
is choral, but I don't believe in harmony. When we all
sing the same notes, we wake a newborn monster.

LIKE EVERYONE ELSE IN THIS WORLD

I was born unarmed, but
by the time I was done
I had developed a rifle
and a wife and a full
set of pall-bearing sons.
In my mid-thirties
I watched a starling
cough up a little blood
and expire on the table.
I'm fond of starlings.
They came to this country
because a naturalist
wanted all of Shakespeare's
birds in the new world.
I think a lot about *King Lear*
and taxidermy, how
The Fool could be
a pelican and King Lear
could be a pelican.
I don't have the proper
equipment, but my other
possessions stun me,
the aproned figurines
I display on the mantel
and more than a dozen
threshers. My will clearly

states the procedures.
If I do not speak,
distribute my licenses
among the retirees.
If I turn away from light,
trim my beard and long hair
and strew the cuttings
in the orchard. This is
an old trick to convince
wild animals that humans
are lurking, just out of sight.

COCORICO

Any time you buy anything,
you should buy an extra, in case
you really like it. I am aware
this makes me sound dumb, like
I am a really dumb shopper.
But buried in my shoulder
is a light that swells constantly
from dim to full-on glow and back
and it provides me with endless
knowledge, like a nutritional syrup
for the astronauts whose mania
for leisure's renowned. Maybe
one day we will be the two
lonely souls forced to sit together
on the Ferris wheel. We will need
a signal. What if when we reach
the top you start humming something
from "The Planets"—then I will know
it's really you and not some radio DJ
trying to give me another prize.
There are a few things I still
have to tell you, like how women
harvest flowers under unfair
conditions and there are members
of my family with less than
perfect hair. Most importantly,

I must convince you that while
it's true I have the face of a human,
this does not make me a centaur,
manticore, or great Icelandic king.
I'm sure you're full of questions,
such as *Have you heard we are*
surrounded by daffodils of normal
proportions? And all I can tell you
is that yes, we are surrounded,
by daffodils, perhaps, but even
more so we are swimming in an air
that's been touched here and there
with the kind of dust that, once
lit up, won't let the swimmers go.

2

BIG SPENDER

All morning my knees were like two roaches
that some bad kid had set on fire and now
it's happening again. I love my neighbor
not even abstractly, for firstly she arranges
about herself a sensible coat. After I was born
I began to understand precisely the devastation
a small event can cause, such as when following
the storm the gazebo in which you'd made love
to countless women collapsed and any hopes
you'd had for summer died suddenly like oddly
frail weeds. Then, as now, you had my sympathy.
I love my car, my lawnmower, my knees which
are still burning. I love systems, like the weather,
and I love to adopt them on Monday and by Thursday
have renounced them altogether. You are older
than eight but too young to enter a pageant
for retirees. I'm a scientist and businessperson,
looking for results. What we are seeking
is a footprint whose physical characteristics—
depth, tread, elapsed time—form an egret so perfect
it seems the very gods patrol the earth.

THE HANDSOME MAN

Walking through the forest I found you,
strapped to a tree and half-fainting.
My god you were beautiful,
your sword sticking out like a sword.
Attempting to revive you, I strutted
around the tree seven times, in
my matchless squirrel coat. You seemed
distracted, though, by the lepers'
parade as they lumbered by, singing
Oh woe is me, my feet are cold,
I cannot find my barrel.
I took off my coat and disguised
myself as a rooster with a cruel eye
and taxable plumage. *There you are, Manfred!*
you said, as your bonds turned to vapor.
You tucked me under your arm
and set out to slay something, while I struggled
to take off your pants with my beak.

GENTLEMAN FARMER

The so-called assassin was, of course,
a washerwoman, a fact so obvious

I died. The funeral arrangements
were their usual mélange

of age-appropriate comedy.
and continental nostalgia,

but when the pallbearers lifted my coffin
and headed out for a night on the town,

a young and gamine mourner exclaimed
That's not Death—that's a box

of lead bells with the tongues removed!
at which point I shoved open the lid,

said *Show's how much you know*
and kissed her on her small, shiny nose.

A moment of awkward silence followed,
during which everyone considered

the huge cost of the gestures they'd made—
the bouquets and stainless steel carafes—

and for a second it seemed they might turn
against me, but then a great light began

to emanate from my all-too-smooth forehead,
informing everyone that peace reigns supreme

in the hearts of all good men,
of which I was one,

and thanks for the memories,
of which I had several,

and please tip the waitstaff
whose poverty's alarming.

VESPERS

When Brian does the homily
I feel like I've just split
the atom, a tiny thing,
and I must hide it from the parish,
so great is my love.
Most things I pretend
never happened. I did not fail
to attach a canoe to the car rack.
The cousin with measles
wasn't mine. In August
I was not the blueberry monster
and also I never met you
by the baggage carousel,
two watering cans in your arms.
There are the growing
and the dying and then
there are your ribbons. As far
as thoughts go, this one is clean.
The geese—all of these
wild geese are beeping.
There's a lack of new reeds
in the lake. The water park
employees have a rich and scary
night life and I want to be let in.
I want to be a local termite and work
for years to wreck the floor.

I do not even know why.
But there is all this fun in method,
pulling blade after blade
from the lawn. No matter
how much I keep breathing,
I cannot see the stars.
It is one of those hopeless cases
from which doctors turn away.
Next Sunday it is your turn
to provide us with refreshments.
Please also grab my hand
and take my pulse. Don't be afraid.
We can say it never happened.
Can claim we were distracted
by the acolyte's green dress.
She will be like a radiant salad.
She will stand on the last plank of youth.

FIVE POEMS FOR AMERICA

I.
Can-can dancing just won't stop
hurting its women. France
is full of stories and women.
Once in Calais three women
lost their money and had
lunch later. Dancing the can-can
shows resilience more clearly
than ever because women have
less money and less strength.
This sounds ugly but my legs
don't want much, except
for clean pants and stuff.

II.
No way is that cowpoke
bringing me home. He wants
someone to fix his religion.
Believe me, I love religion
but he's too quiet when
he's praying. Look, he left
and the bar left and the jukebox
fixed everything. I love this
music and I love this land,
so empty of real trees and hymnals.

III.
Charge! I said, but nobody
heard me, because they were all
listening to their mother, the iPod.
Their mother said a lot of stuff
I didn't hear. Magnificence comes
in a small car, but we all fit.

IV.
Democracy stinks. My classmates
elected the hamster. Teacher
doesn't vote and can't change
anything. Hamsters die all the time
for good reasons. Once I was
a hamster who loved waterparks
but nobody ever knew. Secrets
are also for presidents.
Teacher knows very little.

V.
Northern states. Eastern states.
Where are the armies?
One soldier means trouble.
Five soldiers make a party.
War never means much.
Let's bring the soldiers
somewhere they might like.
Let's go to Pizzeria Uno
and not eat anything.

ACORN DULY CRUSHED

Dear stupid forest.
Dear totally brain-dead forest.
Dear beautiful ugly stupid forest
full of nightingales
why won't you shut up.
What do you want from me.
A train is too expensive.
A clerk will fall asleep.
Dear bitchy stupendous forest.
Trade seats with me.
Now it is your birthday.
Congrats!
Someone will probably slap you
about the face and ears.
Indulgent municipal forest.
Forest of scarves and of beards.
Dear rapid bloodless forest
you are talking all the time.
You are not pithy.
You are like 8,000 swans.
Dear nasty pregnant forest.
You are so hot!
You are environmentally significant.
Men love to hang themselves
from your standard old growth trees.
Don't look at me.

You are the one with
the ancient noble terror.
Bad forest. Forest with
important gangs of leaves.
Dear naïve forest,
what won't you be admitting!
Blunt international forest.
Forest of bees and of hair.
You should come back to my house.
We can bag drugs all night.
You can tell me
about your new windows.
How they are just now
beginning to sprout.

STEP INTO MY WIGWAM

Every day I send the orphans a political message.
I say, *Friends, you may be trying,*
but you are not trying hard enough—
the ceiling is steadily lowering itself and one day
we will return home with our bags of frozen vegetables
to find ourselves utterly crushed.
At least we are living in ingenious times.
I have learned that it's impossible
to smooth out a grave with a rolling pin
and anyway ecology dictates cremation.
I am so fond of this body, esp. my brain
which is full of bees attending
their convention on How to Tame a Nightstick.
They have miniature boxes of corn flakes.
You can eat as many as you'd like.

IT IS RAINING IN HERE

The difference between cross and ball peen
would elude me should I chase it, but it is
of little importance. I am thinking
of the meadow lined with sheep and of
the airport. I am remembering how yesterday
a falcon landed on the telephone pole
and we stepped out of the car, amazed.
It was the color of somebody's carpet.
In somebody's carpet there is a falcon-
shaped hole. The trees here by the airport
stand leafless and wet, full of hidden coils
and a light that battles the asphalt. I love
the asphalt and everyone's terrible behavior.
When I arrived the sheep were already speckling
their areas, but it's a snap to imagine the pleasure
of arranging them at dawn: how they would be
unlikely to stampede. I read once
of a man who suffered from what
they dubbed "phantom antlers"—he'd go
to groom them and instead he'd groom the air.

THE FLEDGLING CROCUS

Soon when I look out the window
there will be light, nothing but.
In Hanover they've detected a weakness.
Thanks a lot, Hanover. This house
is 55 degrees Fahrenheit and frankly
growing colder. Maybe you have
noticed how the saucers of milk
are considering icicles, I think
for the very first time. Who can
resist the call of the inchworm?
Do not even try. Get down
on the floor and get as lucky
as you'd like. Today is the
Holiday of Ill-Begotten Goods.
I stole my pen I stole my land tract.
I am living on someone else's principles.
Hanover, we have greatness
in abundance, we have shivers,
we have fleas. Nest after nest
is abandoned and months from now
when bombed-out children decide
to talk they will each start by reciting
My mother's gorgeous hair...
It is all there. In the short books
of the future. What is here, in this
room, is a small lamp and a vase

that needs changing. Is cubic
space interfered with by hi,
my human form. And there are
other rooms with other forms,
there is a future not prone
to contain me. I am the hundred
and third last telegram. I am sent
with a small degree of urgency stop
please retrieve me from the historic
Empress Hotel. Hanover, let's say
that reading is like grave-rubbing
and the charcoal is your eyes.
Let's say all the things to each other
as if we were two friends chatting
while waiting for the bus. And night
arrives but the bus does not, and a frost
comes on with a mind to disrupt
the fledgling crocus. What can
we spooks do but say thank you—
for our coins and for our progress,
for the kind genetic mutation
that dressed us all those years ago
in warm yet lightweight fur.

ONWARD AND ONWARD

In 1887 the Army Benevolent Fund decided
to charge rent to veterans who cluttered
their otherwise peaceful brains. In 1423
the Indian Ocean demanded respite and
the starfish departed for a spell, vacationed
in Brittany, became the first buttons. Last year
I determined the exact weight of the animals.
They were so grateful they made me mayor.
History's full of recipes & despair. In illustrations
it's a tugboat and we'll all be carried home.
My understanding's incomplete. For instance,
these costumes are clearly stunning, but what's
occurring underneath? No liver would call me
a friend. More importantly, the twentieth century
gave us Chevrolets. We drive around. Even now,
gnawing on the future's lip, I see workers en route
and there is nothing they're not bound to mend.

A BIOGRAPHY OF SOMEONE WE KNOW

The lady had no daughters
seven dresses and a lamp
to constellate the sky.
I am speaking, of course,
of Florence Nightingale,
the Mother of Modern
Nursing. Let's pretend
to be soldiers dying.
Now we love her so much
she can't move to dress
our wounds or keep
records. Now we've
invented photography.
Let's think again
about war. Everything
breaks out like it. Parks
and rough embraces. Anything
to give us a new explanation
for scars. For the weather
we have no explanation
worth keeping. If Florence
comes we'll entertain her
with elaborate cloud histories.
It's thanks to her that
we're even a little famous.
Tourists will come to stand

on our graves and say things.
It's hard to hear them.
They're looking for saints.
Christ, all I can think of
is peeling off her skirts.
Her petticoats, white
and useless. A little damp.
Where will our courage go,
our lips, our poor fingers.

3

BARNSTORMER

I do not have a farm do you have
a farm? on my farm are horses
cows pigeons chickens a dungeon
they tend to themselves it's so easy!
I do not feel well do you feel
well? my throat's on fire I mean
missing something crucial let's say
the filament say *filament!* everyone
feels really good especially the horses
riding around like a bunch of stupid
chickens those are some foxy
beasts! I think beauty rises from
the dead do you think beauty rises?
like the great retarded sun? like
here comes beauty with its slow
dumb light and it's touching stuff
& now I'm scattering feed I ordered
from mother nature's catalog
which everyone knows has the best
pictures that's why it's all cut up
& the seed is falling out the holes &
the chickens are falling out
the holes & everyone gets papercuts!
goodbye chickens have a nice
time exploding in oblivion!

BECAUSE THE LIMIT SEEKS ITS OWN

It's not enough to bring forth witnesses to some
impending crime—when goslings die the nation
gets sadder. Who can afford to desert our small
unfriendly comrades? If I had two more dollars
or daughters, I'd be another lonely surgeon with
dreams of calling home. Bronchitis, pneumonia
& yellow fever make everyone taller, like adolescent
trees. Trees here do a job like any other: morning,
teatime, nightcaps with strangers. Name one
building. If it's blue, keep going. How many
men want to go home. There are so many
reasons they can't and mostly the dust. What
doesn't it get into. And all day long the sweeping
and candor that can't prevent the babe from falling
in the tub. So happily floating when you come
to take her out. I don't mean happy and dead,
I mean surviving in a way that removes your
tongue from your mouth, your heart from its
cage and lastly spills your loins all over your
tiles like love or some brighter cement.

BECAUSE THERE ARE NO FAMILIES

But what I actually put an end to is my belief
in what can be undone: murder, education,
the birth of some new species. I put them all
in a basket that can be ignored but not destroyed.
Weddings seem increasingly outrageous, something
in the centerpieces and vows toward a final
cleanliness. Who knew I'd be alone here
on a frivolous grassy hump, chilled as much
as I, a felon, do deserve. Electricity exists
for only those who need it. I am one. I need it
for my architecture and my desire. When I look
at people's crotches, my face is finally beautiful.
I should not breed. Should not marry or start
an agricultural movement. I'd call it fruitful
devastation and so would my followers. What
would we live on? We'd live on modification,
the remainder when the divisor tastes sweet.
I have an expiration date. It's stamped in
the pretty nice bones of my inner ear. Everyone's
born in the park, where tourists get grains
of rice engraved. We can't remember everything,
just the money we give to strangers when their
need elevates us to a charitable team. When is
the next available appointment? When can we
expect to actually sleep? Try again later. Try
again later. Try turning to your left, to your belly,
like a body. I wonder if you hurt your body.

ROUGH SCIENCE

But stars do not stay hot.
They freeze and drop

into our soft drinks. It is
a way they have of dying

without becoming sad.
Husband and I have agreed

to a trial separation. (Why
I am sleeping on the roof.)

Today I am going
to think about moss.

Moss so handsome that
when I see it I want to take

a nap, a nap immediately.
And I will sleep forever

until the friends arrive and
wake me with their clinking

and it is the Fourth of July
and it has been for months.

TELEVISION

People like surprises.
Surprise! I am your uncle.
And that kind of thing.
Or they would rather refill
the ice trays for eight hours
a day. A job is a job.
If you cut your bangs short
you'll look more constantly
surprised. At school, at
the funeral. I didn't know
him well, but he was my uncle.
Some people call close friends
uncle. Sometimes people
call each other to make sure
they didn't die in the flood.
If you are having an emergency
call 911. 999 if you are
the English. That would be
a surprise. If you stand outside
the bathroom to surprise me
with your own concertina,
I will scream. Please don't
be alarmed. Car alarms surprise
nobody. Nobody, you surprise me,
how you are always sneaking in.
Ladies & gentlemen, Uncle Nobody.
Nobody, this is your life.

HAT DANCE COMMA MEXICAN

I am certain that you have a head,
for I have spoken with it daily

when we discuss the weather,
and listen, the weather is good.

It is totally necessary. Would you
accuse me of keeping tornadoes

in my pants? I think it could
really help me in my next audition.

I want to be Storm Team #4.
I have the acting bug and

the cumulonimbus bug.
And I'm not even scared.

Look, you are using your head
to bite me. That ought to be

proof enough. Maybe you
would like a drink? Beside

the constant downpours, this is
the driest state I've lived in. And

somehow full of, what is it,
shelves. That's not an invitation

to go climbing. Here, lie down
on top of the armoire. It is

a big one. Meanwhile, I will play
a demonstration game of I Spy.

I spy, with my little eye,
the German city of Hamburg.

I've given it away. Despite
my mistake, I think you've

got the picture. Well, let's
tunnel down to Zanzibar. And

now we are in Zanzibar, which
you don't like one bit. I can tell

by the way you are not breathing.
I think this powder will revive you.

I bought it from a local merchant.
Now you are quite well. Now you are,

what, made of sand? And leaking.
You are a taxing companion.

If anyone is chasing us they will
surely track us down. Already

I can hear them, their horses
and their wives. I suppose if

it were up to you we'd join them.
You always want to be marauders.

THE AVALANCHE CLUB

The article said it helps to look for one thing,
as a way of accidentally discovering something else.
I picked bears. I was looking for bears.

It didn't work. I mean
all I ever got was bears.

The secretary at the elementary school
which had recently seceded
from the Governor Wentworth District
was a bear, and also a steamboat enthusiast.

At the gallery
I saw a miniature daguerreotype
of a bear reclining naked
on a mossy embankment.

I was reminded of my childhood ballet teacher,
her elegant teeth.

I complained to my friends.
I said I am looking for bears
and I am finding them everywhere
but I am not finding, for example,
a town in Tennessee

populated entirely by historians
who refute the Persian Wars.

My friends looked at one another
and ordered a new round

while at the back of the room
a bear in a tiny car
drove in circles on the platform.

Maybe you have a similar problem.
Maybe for you it's phone booths
which you chose for their disappearance
and their mostly romantic history.

When I arrived at the motel room
the bear was already there, shivering,
because of the air conditioner
which we could not control.

All night long the television
broadcast interviews on hibernation.
At three I fell asleep, informed.

ONE OF SEVERAL TALKING MEN

Because my head is a magnet for bullets
I am spending the day indoors. First

I admired the topiary for several hours
and when my eyes began to ache I rang

for lunch. Lunch arrived with injunctions.
I considered my feet. I did not consider

my altitude. Because I stuffed myself
into the reliquary, I am finding movement

difficult. Luckily, I would not dream
of dancing in this outfit. You must be

a foreign exchange student. Allow me
to make an observation: We live beneath

a frugal moon, and only in her bad light
do our women seem consumptive.

Though what do I know. I am, moreover,
a senatorial moment, and if you don't

forget me, I may do it myself. You could
conceivably think I've never known love,

but I suspect that in the war years, when nurses
bandaged my wounds with repetitive flair,

there existed between us if not affection,
at least a sense that the subject could arise.

WILDERNESS WITH TWO MEN

Some of the trees looked like snakes
and it was dangerous to step on them.
We were going somewhere,
somewhere important,
and we were in love,
but not with each other.
We spoke with little smoke
signals we picked up
at a trading post,
but we were running
low on every phrase except
those concerning the weather,
so these were our words
for affection, hunger and loss.
At the mouth of the river
we had to part and reunite
with our enormous wives and families.
We divided up the supplies:
tin cans, rope, rocks
shaped like women,
lighter fluid and dice,
building two neat piles on either bank,
and then stood across from one another,
taking shots at what
we thought were different clouds.

STROKING MY HEAD
WITH MY DECEPTION STICK

Someone shut down the local shimmer
but not the police who thought

it was Sunday and so spent hours
arranging their long and pliant hair.

Constable Jacques is the best man I know
but even he won't converse with the dead.

The dead are so vain and hungry—
they will straddle your mirrors and swallow

your oak trees with their huge elastic lips.
And then you hear the screaming, not to be found

within the dead, but rather in the tiny
black pot which holds the greater part

of our mass and the difficult
farm where all the hens are black

and black are the wheatfields through which
runs a black and silent wind. Thin teachers

explain to our children: if the farm is a burgeoning
snowglobe, then the screaming's a legend, like glass.

4

AFTER DINNER THEY RETIRED
TO THE LIBRARY

I cannot keep you here much longer.
What we have already eaten
gathers its bones and deposits
itself in the trash. Thank you.
No, thank you. I have not read
a pamphlet of such delicacy
for weeks, and even then it seemed
my eyes were dangling in the past.
We are not wealthy. We do not
know why our mothers love
to tear apart the ceiling.
What wild treasure have we missed?
I would spin around forever
if I thought we could move forward,
though my assignment is to drill
down through the floorboards,
chatting with the dead as they go by.
Oh weather. Oh mathematics.
Oh total lack of plans for deprivation.
We have seen a wily tiger stalk the hallway,
but there is no spare time to tame it.
We are only one man, and he's asleep.

WHATEVER DOESN'T ARRIVE WILL LATER

But perhaps we are getting ahead of ourselves—let's say
    our thinking
is a fun car our noses are attached to. In thirty years the
    sun will have

pulled off a lot of dirty tricks and not been punished.
    Other things
you can't arrest are: leaves and crazy loving. The leaves
    arrived

all at once this year, came on like a clumsy chorus. *Hi!*
    We're all here
in our outfits! It is hard to dislike the trees, but we should
    probably

try, as a kind of exercise or basic amusement. We could
    do it for hours
and arrange for someone to stop by with a sandwich.
    Yesterday, today,

tomorrow, we must eat eat eat! Which is but one of many
    things
that ducks say to their offspring. Learning can take place
    anywhere—

the parking lot, Milan, the parking garage. It's all a matter
    of close
regard for the gasoline-lipped puddle. And then a spring
    into action,

a sprint into *plein air,* where all the wives have gathered. They are
  of infinite variety, some lacquered, some even giving off mist, having

only just left the aquarium, where they spent days with the kids touching
starfish. Let's go up and introduce ourselves—speak whatever language

comes to mind—they cannot hear us, but need only a little opening
through which it becomes polite to smile and offer us their hand.

A BETTER POETRY CONCERNING MY MOTHER

It is difficult, a good poetry concerning my mother.
She is generally done right to a cap.
Commitment to the dead wants of the sun!
Even when you shout that, it is still not easy,
a good poetry concerning my mother,
because underneath the straw she is almost too much
or to outside my britches have escaped, stamped
like in my average ear. Ow and ow.
Goedendag, mummy!
I become concerned penetrating shouts and the woman
in Canada deeply saddens—must be, she has
no regrets and she sings herself outside
the shower, no regrets and she does soap her thighs.

UNTO US A HOLIDAY

When the light would not conform to levels
specified on the reflective packaging, an attorney
arrived to treat us to a consolation dinner.
The maître d' cannot forget us, hard as he might
roll himself into the municipal sandpit, from which
come the beaches! And the population strolls in
with a canoe. By now you know I love you
as a mother loves her somersaulted skier:
you are cold, you say little, but over your
charming red jacket I embrace you fiercely
as my own and can only hope this is not
another tragicomic instance of misplaced
recognition. Dogs are always going home
with a new and potentially superior family,
beginning the month as calmly as a sherpa
on leave. Everyone needs a vacation. If
it is not you, I apologize truly and invite you
to depart with this fruit basket, a token
of my strident esteem. Was there once a man
who, having stepped on a train in the wrong
direction, rode all the way to Mattapan, due
to his impeccable sense of transportational
obligation? I hope so, for if he did, then
the furthering of impromptu splendor could
have only increased when from behind
he thought a resident of this new town

resembled particularly his handsome wife.
The world is fond of us, with reservation.
A pair of ducks will nap on the asphalt.
And if your ticket's gone missing or you think
the map has systematically disarrayed itself
each time the light hit its junctions, then
we will compose together a note shedding
grace on your troubles and wait in old-fashioned
quiet for your generous forthcoming reward.

UPON THE RIVER PANG

The natural look of the village isn't changing me,
just building a frame in which church bells
can start ringing to announce one wedding
and seventeen births, including a future leader
of this, our native state. I call the chickens names.
I call them to sit near me in the middle of all this air
and the rural population. If a farmer wants something
to do with me there is a way for him to get it.
A public footpath, so to speak, by which I mean
my bloodline. Once in a tree I saw a roughness
that scoured the eye to a new kind of friction,
catching not on branches, but rather on the sky
they scraped out. Turns out it was a disease
the farmer was learning to prevent. There are
injections too sultanic for me to bring up
in town meeting and so instead I suggest knitting
a sort of agricultural scroll. Or party officials
could sanction some new interpretations of yarn.
There is nothing happening now except a stirring
in the hayfield, which even the sheep can't explain.
Red, gold, contusion—there are so many appropriate
colors in my recent floral arrangements that I almost
think I've cheated, but a quick review of the inventory
and yet another breath confirm it is merely the land
proffering order to oppose this ad hoc rain.

THE BARBARIST

I wanted to stomp around the room
shouting at the orioles, but I have to
act now on an amazing offer
or I will spend the rest of eternity
kicking myself in the face
with my genuine cowboy boots.
Come in Mr. Roosevelt, Mr. Adams,
Mr. Didn't-Feel-Obligated-to-Wear-Any-Pants.
Where are your bustling wives?
I wanted to offer you my heart,
but I have to lead the nation through
this cold and open valley. Forgive me,
you have pudding all over your beard,
you look a downright ass. Darlings!
You are here at my invitation and
for that I am totally confused.
Life could not get any better
and then it did, and then there was
a mild famine, and now whom
can we knight for their service?
You—hold this bucket of milk.
And you—emerge from darkness.
Now stand and shake that butt as though
some god were shaking it for you.

PALE LEMON SQUARE

When they say nobody rides horses anymore
what they mean is: *look, the ineffable sadness
has returned,* and while every mindless plant
in town is blooming, an accidental family
reunion is also growing, and my neighbors'
houses are filling up with maiden aunts.
For a time, trading was all the rage, and now
I'd like to try it again. You give me
your native handbag collection, and I will give you
my lilac soap. Later we can get carried away
and perhaps even employ a tombola. I will not,
I cannot remain in charge of prizes. Please,
you must look quickly at our fellow citizens
and tell me, do they not seem unwell? I feel so
concerned. I feel like I've been studying
to become a doctor forever and now, faced
with a real-world pandemic, I'm full
of unmitigated lust for business—as though
I were sitting in a high school classroom
watching the morning's snow foster impending
cancellations and all the attendant policies. Soon,
if not at once, the library and gymnasium will be
redubbed infirmaries, and you and I will drift
among the cots like swans in ever-wider grids.

THE LONG DIVIDER

I.
I found a notebook in which
someone had written directions
for memorizing fortune cookies
in the order you receive them,
but I knew the future was already
almost over. A scientist was speculating
on the radio about a point of view
known as "the fifth person,"

and everyone in the waiting room
became mildly indignant, except
one nurse for whom this new theory
was practically a religion. She drew
strength from it when she was not drawing
blood for a full battery of diagnostic tests.

I did not feel especially sick. My head
was about eight feet from the ceiling.

II.
On the train I sat facing
everything we were leaving behind,
the irrevocable rebuilding
of a roughly historic district.

When we paused and all the lights
and fans clicked off I could hear
the nearby soldiers breathing.

Somewhere in Ohio I fell asleep
against the window and dreamt
myself into a trial-size affair.

III.
My blood and lungs had been
adjusted so that the new levels
would make my impoverished brain
read everything as an emergency.

They were all bright blue, stunning
and coming at me like a bag
of perfect marbles.

Standing at the intersection,
happily attacked by WALK,
I pawed around for a way to calm
the policeman who wanted
to protect and serve me.
It's the pigeons, I said,
I'm seeing just the right amount.

IV.
A large manila envelope
was waiting for me at home.
It was a message from the nurse.

She said my lucky numbers
were 4, 12, 17 and 38.

She said the Chinese word for bear.

V.
Later that evening I moved my tent
into the hallway and made eyes
on the wall with two flashlights.
I started drawing saplings
near the floorboards, but
it was going to take forever.

The hallway wasn't cold enough
to invite anyone to join me
in the dark blue sleeping bag.
I would have to run the icemaker all night.

VI.
At four a.m. the pharmacy was like a theme park
whose theme was Being Very Quiet.
When I stepped back outside
the sun was glaring at our horizon.

I planned out what I would say
when the television news teams arrived.
It was as if since the beginning of time
a pelican had been hurtling through space
with a torch in his beak and at last
he could hold it no longer.

I sat on the sidewalk to wait for them.
They would drive up in golden vans.

ACKNOWLEDGEMENTS

Thank you to the editors of the following journals in which these poems first appear, sometimes in slightly different form:

Bateau, "What an Undertaker Does to His Family at Night."

Boston Review, "Acorn Duly Crushed."

Glitterpony, "One of Several Talking Men."

Invisible Ear, "Pale Lemon Square."

Linebreak, "The Avalanche Club," and "Onward and Onward."

LIT, "Hat Dance Comma Mexican," "Rough Science," and "What Is the Croup."

Notnostrums, "The Fledgling Crocus," and "Vespers."

Octopus, "Five Poems for America," "Not My Native Tongue," and "Wilderness with Two Men."

The Pebble Lake Review, "A Biography of Someone We Know."

Pilot, "A Better Poetry Concerning My Mother," "Unto Us a Holiday," and "Whatever Doesn't Arrive Will Later."

Sixth Finch, "Cocorico," and "It Is Raining in Here."

Tarpaulin Sky, "Themselves Performing Small Brave Acts."

Third Coast, "Stroking My Head with My Deception Stick."

Verse, "Barnstormer," "Because the Limit Seeks Its Own," and "Because There Are No Families."

Heartfelt thanks to the good people whose encouragement, suggestions and friendship helped me to make these poems:

Josh Bolton, Bill Cassidy, Michael Christle, Michele Christle, Valerie Schurer Christle, Carson Cistulli, Christina Clark, Lyndsey Cohen, Noah Feehan, Jeannie Hoag, Seth Landman, Lisa Olstein, Nat Otting, Seth Parker, Natalie Lyalin, Emily Pettit, Zachary Schomburg, Mathias Svalina, Jim Tate, Emily Toder, and Dara Wier.

Thanks also and endlessly to Christopher DeWeese.